QUIET TIMES
with
CHARLES
SPURGEON

A Life Essentials Journal

QUIET TIMES
with
CHARLES
SPURGEON

COMPILED AND INTRODUCED
BY JAMES S. BELL, JR.

MOODY PRESS
CHICAGO

All Scripture quotations, unless otherwise indicated, are taken from the New King James Version. Copyright © 1979, 1980, 1982 by Thomas Nelson, Inc. Used by permission. All rights reserved.

Scripture quotations marked KJV are taken from the King James Version.

Library of Congress Cataloging-in-Publication Data

Spurgeon, C.H. (Charles Haddon), 1834–1892.
    Quiet times with Charles Spurgeon / compiled and introduced by James S. Bell, Jr.
       p. cm.
    ISBN ISBN 0-8024-7048-3
     1. Meditations. I. Bell, James S. II. Title
    BV4832.2 S746 2000
    242--dc21

                                                              00-056114

                    1 3 5 7 9 10 8 6 4 2

             Printed in the United States of America

To Daniel Barker,
who takes solid preaching seriously

CONTENTS

INTRODUCTION

*E*ach year hundreds of brand-new Christian books appear not only in Christian bookstores but, increasingly, in secular bookstores and even in retail chain stores throughout the country. It is exciting to see so many topics addressed from a Christian point of view, reaching such a large potential audience with a message of hope and truth.

Though it is important to be relevant and contemporary, this trend may also tend to obscure the fact that there is a huge wealth of Christian classics written over a century ago which are available to help us grow in areas far more important—in the essentials of our relationship with God.

The latest publishing trends may address issues rarely touched upon in the past: taking care of your physical health, raising your teenager, or even the ethics of genetic engineering. But the basics of our relationship with God never change, and it is here, in our response to His love and commandments, where our greatest needs lie, whether they are felt or not.

Our greatest challenges lie in understanding the teachings found in His Word, obeying them, and bearing fruit consistent with the nature and purposes of Christ. It is in these areas that classic Christian works excel. At times we may find that the essentials of the faith get pushed to the periphery in our Christian reading and may be covered superficially even in our devotional life.

One advantage the classics retain in books related to the "Christian living" or "spiritual growth" categories is that they have withstood the scrutiny of succeeding generations. The fruit of the ministries of such great preachers as D.L. Moody, Andrew Murray, and Charles Spurgeon included the conversion of countless thousands of souls as well as strengthening the maturity and impact of the church here and abroad.

The various volumes of Moody, Spurgeon, and Murray have sold millions of copies in numerous editions, and most titles remain on bookstore shelves today. Perhaps one reason for this is that their main target was not the educated elite but the masses. They geared the message of the Gospel to be understood by the average working-class person of the time, and thus their style, by and large, is not archaic today.

I do not mean to imply that they shied away from in-depth biblical knowledge, but rather that they communicated in a simple and straightforward manner as men who truly "knew their Bibles" and had a passion for the average Christian to grow to his or her full stature in Christ.

The preaching and the writings that follow in this Quiet Times series are designed to shake you out of your spiritual lethargy and challenge you to live a life of deeply committed discipleship. They continually focus on the great love of God in Christ and yet specify the need to be like Him and separate from the world. This series is not for complacent Christians who want to merely feel better and enhance the quality of their private lives, but those who want to embark upon the exciting adventure of surrendering all to God. Staying with the essentials, their topics include abiding in Christ, servanthood, prayer, the meaning of the Gospel, the character of God, repentance, and other central teachings and practices at the heart of our walk with God.

Perhaps what makes this series most distinctive is its format. These three great preachers promoted the spiritual disciplines in their ministries, and they wholeheartedly supported biblical meditation and prayer, as well as the application of biblical principles—all of which are found in this journal format.

With the introduction of the LifeEssentials journals that comprise the Quiet Times series, I have attempted to bring together two means of getting closer to God. Most journals today consist of blank pages where we articulate our deepest prayers and monitor our spiritual progress. Yet there is no immediate inspiring text to respond to and record our understanding.

At the same time, solid Christian books of the Moody-Murray-Spurgeon variety allow no room for devotional activity: the opportunity to write prayers, express our understanding of key elements of the text, and make commitments to these same principles. The LifeEssentials journals combine text, prayers, questions, and goals in order to offer the reader a high-quality and satisfying devotional experience.

This book, *Quiet Times with Charles Spurgeon,* features the writings and words of Charles Spurgeon, widely known as "the prince of preachers" in the nineteenth century. Spurgeon was a pastor of London's Metropolitan Tabernacle Church. The fifty-two selections can be read daily, occasionally, or weekly. If you choose the latter option, you may wish to record somewhere else how well you achieved your spiritual goals that week.

However you decide to use this journal, it is my profound hope that you will not only have touched the heart of this great preacher and evangelist, but in your quiet moments alone, will have touched the heart of God.

This series is the first release of a forthcoming imprint entitled *LifeEssentials Books*. These books will concentrate on the priorities found at the intersection between faith and living. Based upon what we learn about God and His commands in Scripture, we will be able to better respond in all the critical areas of our lives by being renewed in His image in true holiness.

James S. Bell Jr.
Executive Editor
LifeEssentials Books

SPIRITUAL BLINDNESS

1

Likewise you also, reckon yourselves to be dead indeed to sin,
but alive to God in Christ Jesus our Lord.
ROMANS 6:11

Man is by nature blind within. The Cross of Christ, so laden with glories, and glittering with attractions, never attracts him, because he is blind and cannot see its beauties. Talk to him of the wonders of the creation, show to him the many-colored arch that spans the sky, let him behold the glories of a landscape, he is well able to see all these things; but talk to him of the wonders of the covenant of grace, speak to him of the security of the believer in Christ, tell him of the beauties of the Person of the Redeemer, and he is quite deaf to all your description. You are as one that plays a goodly tune, it is true; but he regards not, he is deaf, he has no comprehension.

I ask, do you find your power equal to your will? You could say, even at the bar of God Himself, that you are sure you are not mistaken in your willingness. You are willing to be wrapped up in devotion; it is your will that your soul should not wander from a pure contemplation of the Lord Jesus Christ, but you find that you cannot do that, even when you are willing, without the help of the Spirit. Now, if the quickened child of God finds a spiritual inability, how much more the sinner who is dead in trespasses and sin?

RESPONDING IN PRAYER

"Lord, the wonders of Your work in Christ far surpass
any earthly wonders we may behold. Help me to see with
my spiritual eyes the glory of Your salvation."

Continuing in prayer . . .

_____

_____

_____

_____

_____

FOR REFLECTION

What parts of God's Word do you have a particularly hard time understanding?
How can the Holy Spirit help your understanding? (See John 16:7–14 as you answer this question.)

_____

_____

_____

_____

_____

_____

_____

_____

_____

_____

_____

SPIRITUAL GOALS FOR THE WEEK

_____

_____

_____

_____

_____

_____

_____

_____

SIMPLE FAITH

| 2 |

For the grace of God that brings salvation has appeared to all men.
TITUS 2:11

$\mathcal{G}$od works in providence, but men do not therefore sit still. They could not move without the divine power giving them life and strength, and yet they proceed upon their way without question, the power being bestowed from day to day by Him in whose hand their breath is, and whose are all their ways. So is it in grace. We repent and believe, though we could do neither if the Lord did not enable us. We forsake sin and trust in Jesus, and then we perceive that the Lord has caused us to will and to do of His own good pleasure. It is idle to pretend that there is any real difficulty in the matter.

Some truths which are hard to explain in words are simple enough in actual experience. There is no discrepancy between the truth that the sinner believes and that his faith is wrought in him by the Holy Spirit. Only folly can lead men to puzzle themselves about plain matters while their souls are in danger. No man would refuse to enter a lifeboat because he did not know the specific gravity of bodies; neither would a starving man decline to eat till he understood the whole process of nutrition. If you will not believe till you can understand all mysteries, you will never be saved at all; and if you allow self-invented difficulties to keep you from accepting pardon through your Lord and Savior, you will perish in a condemnation which will be richly deserved.

RESPONDING IN PRAYER

"Lord, Your truth is not as difficult as we sometimes make it,
but we may simply not want to obey it.
Give us the simple faith to both understand and obey."

Continuing in prayer . . .

_____

_____

_____

_____

_____

_____

When have the "hard sayings" of Jesus caused you to shrink back from the ultimate implications of radical obedience? Yet, what do you miss when not following Him to that extent?

_____

_____

_____

_____

_____

_____

_____

_____

_____

_____

_____

SPIRITUAL GOALS FOR THE WEEK

_____

_____

_____

_____

_____

_____

_____

_____

_____

A WEALTHY PARTNERSHIP

3

I have been crucified with Christ; it is no longer I who live,
but Christ lives in me.

GALATIANS 2:20

*D*well much upon this partnership with the Son of God, unto which you have been called, for all your hope lies there. You can never be poor while Jesus is rich because you are in one firm with Him. Want can never assail you, since you are joint-proprietor with Him who is possessor of heaven and earth. You can never fail, for though one of the partners in the firm is as poor as a church mouse and in himself an utter bankrupt who could not pay even a small amount of his heavy debts, yet the other Partner is inconceivably, inexhaustibly rich.

In such a partnership you are raised above the depression of the times, the changes of the future, and the shock of the end of all things. The Lord has called you into the fellowship of His Son Jesus Christ, and by that act and deed He has put you into the place of infallible safeguard.

If you are indeed a believer, you are one with Jesus, and therefore you are secure. Do you not see that it must be so? You must be confirmed to the end until the day of His appearing, if you have indeed been made one with Jesus by the irrevocable act of God. Christ and the believing sinner are in the same boat; unless Jesus sinks, the believer will never drown. Jesus has taken His redeemed into such connection with Himself that He must first be smitten, overcome, and dishonored before the least of His purchased ones can be injured.

RESPONDING IN PRAYER

"Lord, help me to realize that I have all I need in my partnership with
Jesus. I seek to better acquire these riches by faith and obedience."

Continuing in prayer . . .

Thank God for the total and eternal security you have in Him even when everything else of an earthly nature fails.

_____

_____

_____

_____

_____

_____

_____

_____

_____

_____

SPIRITUAL GOALS FOR THE WEEK

_____

_____

_____

_____

_____

_____

_____

_____

_____

_____

_____

THE WATCHTOWER OF PRAYER

---| 4 |---

Then He spoke a parable to them,
that men always ought to pray and not lose heart.

LUKE 18:1

*O*ur Lord meant by saying men ought always to pray, that they ought to be always in the spirit of prayer, always ready to pray—like the old knights always wearing their weapons where they could readily reach them, and always ready to encounter wounds or death for the sake of the cause which they championed. Those grim warriors often slept in their armor; so even when we sleep we are still to be in the spirit of prayer, so that if perchance we wake in the night we may still be with God.

Our soul, having received the divine centripetal influence which makes it seek its heavenly center, should be evermore naturally rising towards God himself. Our heart is to be like those beacons and watchtowers which were prepared along the coast of England when the invasion of the Armada was hourly expected, not always blazing, but with the wood always dry, and the match always there, the whole pile being ready to blaze up at the appointed moment.

Our souls should be in such a condition that expressive prayer should be frequent. No need to pause in business and fall down upon the knees; the spirit should send up its silent, short, swift petition to the throne of grace.

RESPONDING IN PRAYER

"Lord, may I always be ready to pray on every occasion where it would benefit me and allow You to work in a greater way in my life."

Continuing in prayer . . .

_____

_____

_____

_____

_____

_____

_____

How can you better learn to pray without ceasing even in the busy activities of life? Consider some steps you can take to either clear time or become alert to prayer opportunities throughout the day.

_____

_____

_____

_____

_____

_____

_____

_____

_____

_____

SPIRITUAL GOALS FOR THE WEEK

_____

_____

_____

_____

_____

_____

_____

_____

_____

TRUTH OR COUNTERFEIT?

5

Do not love the world or the things in the world.
If anyone loves the world, the love of the Father is not in him.
1 JOHN 2:15

This age is full of shams. If you walked through the streets of London, you might imagine that all the shops were built of marble, and that all the doors were made of mahogany and woods of the rarest kinds; and yet you soon discover that there is scarce a piece of any of these precious fabrics to be found anywhere, but that everything is grained, painted and varnished. I find no fault with this, except that it is an outward type of an inward evil that exists.

As it is in our streets, so it is everywhere: graining, painting, and gilding are at an enormous premium. Counterfeit has at length attained to such an eminence that it is with the utmost difficulty that you can detect it. Specially is this the case in religious matters. There was once an age of intolerant bigotry, when every man was weighed in the balance, and if he was not precisely up to the orthodox standard of the day, the fire devoured him; but in this age of charity, and of most proper charity, we are very apt to allow the counterfeit to pass, and to imagine that outward show is really as beneficial as inward reality. If ever there was a time when it was needful to say, "Beware of the leaven of the Pharisees, which is hypocrisy," it is now.

RESPONDING IN PRAYER

"Lord, I want my devotion to You to be the authentic
rather than mere outward appearance. Examine my heart
and see if there is any hypocrisy within me."

Continuing in prayer . . .

_____

_____

_____

_____

_____

How might you better allow Christ to live His life in you rather than you trying to put on a show?

_____
_____
_____
_____
_____
_____
_____
_____
_____
_____

SPIRITUAL GOALS FOR THE WEEK

_____
_____
_____
_____
_____
_____
_____
_____
_____
_____

ALL SUFFICIENCY

6

And He said to me, "My grace is sufficient for you,
for my strength is made perfect in weakness."

2 CORINTHIANS 12:9

The other evening I was riding home after a heavy day's work. I felt very wearied and sore depressed, when swiftly and suddenly as a lightening flash, the text came to me, "My grace is sufficient for you." I reached home and looked it up in the original, and at last it came to me in this way, "*My* grace is sufficient for you"; and I said, "I should think it is, Lord," and burst out laughing. I never fully understood what the holy laughter of Abraham was until then. It seemed to make unbelief so absurd. It was as though some little fish, being very thirsty, was troubled about drinking the river dry, and Father Thomas said, "Drink away, little fish, my stream is sufficient for you." Or, it seemed after the seven years of plenty, a mouse feared it might die of famine; and Joseph might say, "Cheer up, little mouse, my granaries are sufficient for you."

Again, I imagined a man away up yonder, in a lofty mountain, saying to himself, "I breathe so many cubic feet of air every year, I fear I shall exhaust the oxygen in the atmosphere," but the earth might say, "Breathe away, O man, and fill the lungs ever, my atmosphere is sufficient for you."

Oh, brethren, be great believers! Little faith will bring your souls to heaven, but great faith will bring heaven to your souls.

RESPONDING IN PRAYER

"Lord, help me to drink of the waters of life and realize there is no end to Your mercy and love, no matter how I feel or what I've done."

Continuing in prayer . . .

_____

_____

_____

_____

_____

Seek God for more provision in every area of need in your life. What is holding
back your faith from receiving his bounty that is meant for you?

_____

_____

_____

_____

_____

_____

_____

_____

_____

_____

SPIRITUAL GOALS FOR THE WEEK

_____

_____

_____

_____

_____

_____

_____

_____

_____

_____

GO TELL IT

$$\boxed{7}$$

Therefore comfort one other with these words.
1 THESSALONIANS 4:18

*H*ow much might we tell of what the Lord has done for us personally! Here is a subject that shall never be exhausted. Talk to one another, especially to those who can understand you because they have felt the same, of the longsuffering of God when you were in your ungodly state; the wonders of that love which tracked you with its many warnings while you were still strangers to yourselves and to God. Talk of that Almighty power which, when the predestinated honor had come, laid hold upon you and made you yield. Speak of what the Lord did for you when you were in the low dungeon of your self-abhorrence; how he met with you when you were brought to death's door; how Jesus appeared for you, and clothed you with his righteousness, and your spirit revived, and your heart was glad.

Shall the slave ever forget the music of his chains when they dropped from his wrists, and will you ever cease to speak of that happy day, the happiest of all days, when all transgression were forever broken off at the love-touch of your Redeemer? Oh no! Talk ye still of the wondrous works of God as connected with your conversion. And, since that time, however quiet your life may have been, I am sure there has been much in it that has tenderly illustrated the Lord's providence, the Lord's guidance, the Lord's deliverance, the Lord's upholding and sustaining you.

RESPONDING IN PRAYER

"Lord, it is impossible to relate in words all that You have done for me, but let me attempt to tell You in prayer and worship and tell others in my testimony."

Continuing in prayer . . .

_____

_____

_____

_____

_____

FOR REFLECTION

Review your greatest strengths and weaknesses in sharing the Gospel. How can you improve on your testimony as well as convincing persuasion of the truth of the Christian faith?

_____

_____

_____

_____

_____

_____

_____

_____

_____

_____

SPIRITUAL GOALS FOR THE WEEK

_____

_____

_____

_____

_____

_____

_____

_____

_____

THE GREATNESS OF HIS MAJESTY

$$8$$

The Lord reigns, He is clothed with majesty;
the Lord is clothed, He has girded Himself with strength.
Surely the world is established, so that it cannot be moved.

PSALM 93:1

We should, before prayer, meditate upon Him to whom it is to be addressed. Let our thoughts be directed to the living and true God. Let me remember that He is omnipotent, then I shall ask large things. Let me remember that He is very tender, and full of compassion, then I shall ask little things and be minute in my supplication. Let me remember the greatness of his covenant, then I shall come very boldly.

Let me remember, also, that His faithfulness is like the great mountains, that His promises are sure to all the seed, then I shall ask very confidently, for I shall be persuaded that He will do as He has said. Let me fill my soul with the reflection of the greatness of His majesty, then I shall be struck with awe; with the equal greatness of his love, then I shall be filled with delight. We could not but pray better than we do if we meditated more before prayer upon the God whom we address.

Then, let me meditate also upon the way through which my prayer is offered; let my soul behold the blood sprinkled on the mercy-seat; before I venture to draw near to God, let me go to Gethsemane and see the Savior as He prays. Let me stand in holy vision at the foot of Calvary and see His body rent, that the veil which parted my soul from all access to God might be rent too, that I might come close to my Father.

RESPONDING IN PRAYER

"Lord, bring me to the place of awe as I contemplate Your majesty, and in doing so fill me with delight as I realize the full extent of Your love."

Continuing in prayer . . .

Define the term "meditation," which goes beyond mere prayer or Bible study. How can you better meditate on both the person of God as well as His Word?

_____

_____

_____

_____

_____

_____

_____

_____

_____

_____

SPIRITUAL GOALS FOR THE WEEK

_____

_____

_____

_____

_____

_____

_____

_____

_____

_____

OUR MARRIAGE PARTNER

"Return, O backsliding children," says the Lord;
"for I am married to you. I will take you, one from a city
and two from a family, and I will bring you to Zion."
JEREMIAH 3:14

*C*hrist Jesus is joined unto His people in marriage union. In love He espoused His church as a chaste virgin, long before she fell under the yoke of bondage. Full of burning affection, He toiled, like Jacob for Rachel, until the whole of her purchase-money had been paid; and now, having sought her by His Spirit, and brought her to know and love Him, He awaits the glorious hour when their mutual bliss shall be consummated at the marriage-supper of the Lamb.

Not yet has the glorious Bridegroom presented His betrothed, perfected and complete, before the Majesty of heaven; not yet has she actually entered upon the enjoyment of her dignities as His wife and queen; she is as yet a wanderer in a world of woe, a dweller in the tents of Kedar; but she is even now the bride, the spouse of Jesus, dear to His heart, precious in His sight, written on His hands, and united with His person. On earth He exercises towards her all the affectionate offices of husband. He makes rich provision for her wants, pays all her debts, allows her to assume His name, and to share in all His wealth. Nor will He ever act otherwise to her. The word "divorce" He will never mention, for "He hates divorce" (Malachi 2:16). Death must sever the conjugal tie between the most loving mortals, but it cannot divide the links of this immortal marriage.

In heaven they marry not, but are as the angels of God, yet there is this one marvelous exception to the rule, for in heaven Christ and His church shall celebrate their joyous nuptials.

RESPONDING IN PRAYER

"Lord, there are so many privileges attached to being Your bride because it is firm and lasting bliss in fellowship with You. Let me look more forward to the great day of the marriage supper of the Lamb."

Continuing in prayer . . .

Though we are the bride of Jesus, we are "wanderers in this world of woe" and the tension is sometimes hard to handle. When you experience trials and the like, how can you still see yourself as Christ's bride?

_____

_____

_____

_____

_____

_____

_____

_____

_____

SPIRITUAL GOALS FOR THE WEEK

_____

_____

_____

_____

_____

_____

_____

_____

_____

SHARING WITH THE POOR

—————— 10 ——————

They desired only that we should remember the poor,
the very thing which I also was eager to do.
GALATIANS 2:10

"The cattle on a thousand hills" are His—He could supply them; He could make the richest, the greatest, and the mightiest bring all their power and riches to the feet of His children, for the hearts of all men are in His control. But He does not choose to do so; He allows them to suffer want, He allows them to pine in penury and obscurity. Why is this? There are many reasons: one is, *to give us, who are favored with enough, an opportunity of showing our love to Jesus.*

We show our love to Christ when we sing of Him, and when we pray to Him; but if there were no sons of need in the world, we should lose the sweet privilege of evidencing our love, by ministering, in almsgiving, to His poorer brethren. He has ordained that thus we should prove that our love stands not in word only, but in deed and in truth. If we truly love Christ, we shall care for those who are loved by Him. Those who are dear to Him will be dear to us.

Let us then look upon it not as a duty, but as a privilege, to relieve the poor of the Lord's flock—remembering the words of the Lord Jesus, "Inasmuch as ye have done it unto one of the least of these My brethren, ye have done it unto Me" (KJV). Surely this assurance is sweet enough, and this motive strong enough, to lead us to help others with a willing hand and a loving heart—recollecting that all we do for His people is graciously accepted by Christ as done to Himself.

RESPONDING IN PRAYER

"Lord, You have made me rich in many ways. Help me to share out of my surplus with those who are poorer than I. Give me a willing hand and a loving heart, loving in deed as well as in truth."

Continuing in prayer . . .

_____

_____

_____

_____

FOR REFLECTION

The poor can mean anyone who is disadvantaged. How are you fulfilling Christ's commands to meet the needs of the poor?

_____

_____

_____

_____

_____

_____

_____

_____

_____

_____

SPIRITUAL GOALS FOR THE WEEK

_____

_____

_____

_____

_____

_____

_____

_____

A HERITAGE IN HEAVEN

—— 11 ——

"And if I go and prepare a place for you, I will come again
and receive you to Myself; that where I am there you may be also."
JOHN 14:3

*Y*ou know that in Solomon's temple there was no sound of hammer heard, for the stones were made ready in the quarries, and brought all shaped and marked so that the masons might know the exact spot in which they were to be placed; so that no sound of iron was needed. All the planks and timbers were carried to their right places, and all the catches with which they were to be linked together were prepared, so that there might not be even the driving of a nail. Everything was ready beforehand.

It is the same with us. When we get to heaven there will be no sanctifying us there, no squaring us with affliction, no hammering us with the rod, no making us fit there. We must be made ready here; and, blessed be His name, Christ will do all that beforehand. When we get there, we shall not need angels to put this member of the church in one place, and that member in another; Christ who brought the stones from the quarry and made them ready, shall Himself place the people in their inheritance in paradise. For He has Himself said: "If I go and prepare a place for you, I will come again and receive you to Myself."

Christ shall be His own usher; He shall receive His people Himself; He shall stand at the gates of heaven Himself to take His own people, and to put them in their allotted heritage in the land of the blessed.

RESPONDING IN PRAYER

"Lord, please be like a potter with the clay: melt me and mold me
to Your own model of what I should be, for I know
that when heaven arrives, Your work will be finished."

Continuing in prayer . . .

_____

_____

_____

_____

What can you do to make God's task easier as the master craftsman who makes you into His image? How have adverse circumstances in your life helped to perfect you?

_____

_____

_____

_____

_____

_____

_____

_____

_____

_____

SPIRITUAL GOALS FOR THE WEEK

_____

_____

_____

_____

_____

_____

_____

_____

_____

_____

RESTORING JOY

12

Restore to me the joy of Your salvation,
and uphold me with Your generous Spirit.
PSALM 51:12

When a believer has fallen into a low, sad state of feeling, he often tries to lift himself out of it by chastening himself with dark and doleful fears. Such is not the way to rise from the dust, but to continue in it. One might as well chain the eagle's wing to make it mount, as doubt in order to increase our grace. It is not the law, but the Gospel which saves the seeking soul at first; and it is not a legal bondage, but Gospel liberty which can restore the fainting believer afterwards. Slavish fear brings not back the backslider to God, but the sweet wooings of love allure him to Jesus' bosom.

Are you this morning thirsting for the living God and unhappy because you cannot find him to the delight of your heart? Have you lost the joy of religion, and is this your prayer, "Restore to me the joy of your salvation"? Are you conscious also that you are barren, like the dry ground; that you are not bringing forth the fruit unto God which He has a right to expect of you; that you are not so useful in the church, or in the world, as your heart desires to be? Then here is exactly the promise which you need, "I will pour water on him who is thirsty" (Isaiah 44:3). You shall receive the grace you so much require, and you shall have it to the utmost reach of your needs.

RESPONDING IN PRAYER

"Lord, I have had my emotional lows at times and my fears of Your displeasure have alienated me from You. Draw me back to You by the sweetness of Your love so that I may not be condemned."

Continuing in prayer . . .

_____

_____

_____

_____

_____

When your commitment to God cools, how might you overcome the obstacles that stand in your way? What initiates this process that should be avoided?

_____

_____

_____

_____

_____

_____

_____

_____

_____

_____

_____

SPIRITUAL GOALS FOR THE WEEK

_____

_____

_____

_____

_____

_____

_____

_____

_____

_____

_____

_____

BANISHING DOUBT

—| 13 |—

Trust in the Lord forever, for . . . the Lord is everlasting strength.
ISAIAH 26:4

$\mathscr{S}$eeing that we have such a God to trust, let us rest upon Him with all our weight; let us resolutely drive out all unbelief, and endeavor to get rid of doubt and fears, which so much mar our comfort; since there is no excuse for fear where God is the foundation of our trust. A loving parent would be sorely grieved if his child could not trust him; and how ungenerous, how unkind is our conduct when we put so little confidence in our heavenly Father, who has never failed us, and who never will!

It were well if doubting were banished from the household of God; but it is to be feared that old Unbelief is as nimble nowadays as when the psalmist asked, "Has His mercy ceased forever? Has His promise failed forevermore?" David had not made any very lengthy trial of the mighty sword of the giant Goliath, and yet he said, "There is none like it." He had tried it once in the hour of his youthful victory, and it had proved itself to be of the right metal, and therefore he praised it ever afterwards; even so should we speak well of our God; there is none like unto Him in the heaven above or the earth beneath: " 'To whom then will ye liken Me, or to whom shall I be equal?' says the Holy One" (Isaiah 40:25).

RESPONDING IN PRAYER

"Lord, doubts and fears continue to assail me and yet there is no God like You—full of mercy and strength. Help me to trust in You with all my heart and give me the assurance I need."

Continuing in prayer . . .

_____

_____

_____

_____

_____

_____

Name your greatest doubts, fears, and even unbelief before the Lord. Look up those verses that prove His trustworthiness and ask God for greater faith.

_____

_____

_____

_____

_____

_____

_____

_____

_____

_____

SPIRITUAL GOALS FOR THE WEEK

_____

_____

_____

_____

_____

_____

_____

_____

_____

PERMANENT BLESSINGS

14

Now this, "Yet once more," indicates the removal
of those things that are being shaken, as of things that are made,
that the things which cannot be shaken may remain.
HEBREWS 12:27

Whatever your losses have been or may be, you enjoy *present salvation*. You are standing at the foot of His cross, trusting alone in the merit of Jesus' precious blood, and no rise or fall of the markets can interfere with your salvation in Him; no breaking of banks, no failures and bankruptcies, can touch that. Then you are *a child of God* this evening. God is your Father. No change of circumstances can ever rob you of *that*. Although by losses brought to poverty, and stripped bare, you can say, "He is my Father still. In my Father's house are many mansions; therefore will I not be troubled."

You have another permanent blessing, namely, *the love of Jesus Christ*. He who is God and Man loves you with all the strength of His affectionate nature—nothing can affect *that*. The fig tree may not blossom, and the flocks may cease from the field; it matters not to the man who can sing, "My Beloved is mine, and I am His." Our best portion and richest heritage we cannot lose.

Whatever troubles come, let us play the man; let us show that we are not such little children as to be cast down by what may happen in this poor fleeting state of time. Our country is Immanuel's land, our hope is above the sky, and therefore, calm as the summer's ocean, we will see the wreck of everything earth-born, and yet rejoice in the God of our salvation.

RESPONDING IN PRAYER

"Lord, no change of earthly circumstances can rob me of You,
so help me not to fear loss. I look forward to my permanent
home in heaven where an imperishable reward awaits me."

Continuing in prayer . . .

_____

_____

_____

_____

Everything that you have in this world belongs to God. Officially hand over the
ownership to everything that you possess and ask God how you can better use it
on His behalf.

_____

_____

_____

_____

_____

_____

_____

_____

_____

_____

_____

SPIRITUAL GOALS FOR THE WEEK

_____

_____

_____

_____

_____

_____

_____

_____

_____

WHITE AS SNOW

15

Purge me with hyssop, and I shall be clean;
wash me, and I shall be whiter than snow.

PSALM 51:7

They who believe in Jesus are as much accepted of God the Father as even His eternal Son is accepted; and they that believe not, let them do what they will. They shall but go about to work out their own righteousness; but they abide under the law, and still shall they be under the curse.

Now, you that believe in Jesus, walk up and down the earth in the glory of this great truth. You are sinners in yourselves, but you are washed in the Blood of Christ. David says, "Wash me, and I shall be whiter than snow" (Psalm 51:7). You have lately seen the snow come down—how clear! how white! What could be whiter? Why, the Christian is whiter than that. You say, "He is black." I know he is as black as anyone—as black as Hell—the blood drop falls on him, and he is as white—"whiter than snow."

The next time you see the snow-white crystals falling from heaven, look on them and say, "Ah! Though I must confess within myself that I am unworthy and unclean, yet, believing in Christ, He hath given me His righteousness so completely, that I am even whiter than the snow as it descends from the treasury of God." Oh, for faith to lay hold on this!

RESPONDING IN PRAYER

"Lord, sometimes I cannot fully comprehend my spotless
condition in Christ. When I sin, please wash me,
and help me to fully confess and repent."

Continuing in prayer . . .

_____

_____

_____

_____

_____

Do you sometimes fail to confess and repent because you don't fully believe that God will totally cleanse you again and again? Talk this over with the Lord.

_____

_____

_____

_____

_____

_____

_____

_____

_____

_____

_____

SPIRITUAL GOALS FOR THE WEEK

_____

_____

_____

_____

_____

_____

_____

_____

_____

_____

FAITH AND FEELINGS

—| 16 |—

For we walk by faith, not by sight.
2 CORINTHIANS 5:7

My worldly troubles press heavily upon me, and sometimes even my spiritual woes are greater than I can bear." Ah, poor soul, let me cast out that stone from thy road. Remember, it is not written, "He that is joyful shall be saved," but "He that *believes* shall be saved." Your faith will make you joyful by and by; but it is as powerful to save you even when it does not make you rejoice. Why, look at many of God's people, how sad and sorrowful they have been! I know they ought not to be. This is their sin; but still it is such a sin that it does not destroy the efficacy of faith. Notwithstanding all the sorrows of the saints, faith still keeps alive, and God is still true to His promise.

Remember, it is not what you feel that saves you; it is what you believe. It is not feeling, but believing. "For we walk by *faith,* not by sight" (2 Corinthians 5:7, italics added). When I feel my soul as cold as an iceberg, as hard as a rock, and as sinful as Satan, yet even then faith ceases not to justify. Faith prevails as truly in the midst of sad feelings as of happy feelings, for then, standing alone, it proves the majesty of its might. Believe, O son of God, believe in Him, and look not for aught in thyself.

RESPONDING IN PRAYER

*"Lord, at times I base my spiritual condition upon my feelings.
I pray that my joy would stem from faith in Your Word
and not upon my transient emotions."*

Continuing in prayer . . .

_____

_____

_____

_____

_____

_____

FOR REFLECTION

Is it possible to have positive feelings but a low faith level? Or vice-versa, to have negative feelings and a high faith level? Explain.

_____

_____

_____

_____

_____

_____

_____

_____

_____

SPIRITUAL GOALS FOR THE WEEK

_____

_____

_____

_____

_____

_____

_____

_____

_____

THE TREE OF LIFE

───────┤ 17 ├───────

In the middle of its street, and on either side of the river, was the tree of life,
which bore twelve fruits, each tree yielding its fruit every month.
And the leaves of the tree were for the healing of the nations.

REVELATION 22:2

To all the inhabitants of heaven the tree of life is equally and perpetually accessible. They may come at it when they may. No cherub's flaming sword stands there to keep them back, but they may always come and eat of its twelve fruits, and pluck its healing leaves.

The leaves of this true *arbor vitae* were for the healing of the nations. Of what can this tree be a type but of our Lord Jesus Christ and His salvation? What can it signify but that the presence of Christ preserves the inhabitants of heaven for ever free from sickness, while beyond heaven—the precincts, among the nations—the saving influence is scattered? As the leaves fall from the trees, so does sacred influence descend from our Lord Jesus in heaven down to the sons of men; and as the leaves are the least precious products of a fruit-bearing tree, so at least things that have to do with Him and come from Him have a healing virtue in them.

The heavenly city is described as *having an abundance of all manner of delights.* Do men rejoice in wealth? The very streets are paved with gold. The gates are pearls and the walls are built of precious stones. No palace of the Caesars or of the Indian Moguls could rival the gorgeous riches of the city of the Great King.

RESPONDING IN PRAYER

"Lord, I thank You that You have made the way open to
the tree of life. Help me to meditate on heaven as my goal
and true home, and feed off of Jesus, who is life eternal."

Continuing in prayer . . .

_____

_____

_____

_____

_____

FOR REFLECTION

What is it about heaven that most motivates you to lead a godly life? Read devotionally Revelation 21:10–22:5, which describe heaven; then respond below.

_____

_____

_____

_____

_____

_____

_____

_____

_____

_____

SPIRITUAL GOALS FOR THE WEEK

_____

_____

_____

_____

_____

_____

_____

_____

_____

_____

ACTS OF FAITH

---| 18 |---

So Jesus said to them, "Because of your unbelief; for assuredly, I say to you, if you have faith as a mustard seed, you will say to this mountain, 'Move from here to there,' and it will move; and nothing will be impossible for you."
MATTHEW 17:20

To sow a mustard seed is a very inexpensive act. Only one grain of mustard: nobody can find me a coin small enough to express its value. I do not know how much mustard seed the man had; certainly it is not a rare thing; but he only took one grain of it, and cast it into his garden. He emptied no bank by that expenditure; and this is one of the excellencies of Sabbath-school work, that it neither exhausts the church of men nor of money. However much of it is done, it does not lessen the resources of our Zion: it is done freely, quietly, without excitement, without sacrifice of life; and yet what a fountain of blessing it is!

Still, it was an act of faith. It is always an act of faith to sow seed; because you have, for the time, to give it up, and receive nothing in return. The farmer takes his choice seed of corn, and he throws it into the soil of his field. He might have made many a loaf of bread with it; but he casts it away. Only his faith saves him from being judged a maniac: he expects it to return to him fiftyfold. We preach and teach as a work of faith; and, remember, it is only as an act of faith that it will answer its purpose. The rule of the harvest is, "According to your faith, let it be to you" (or Matthew 9:29).

RESPONDING IN PRAYER

"Lord, I don't want to hold back but rather take risks of faith without any immediate guarantees. Help me to better sow what I have, that I may reap a harvest later."

Continuing in prayer . . .

_____

_____

_____

_____

_____

What talents, time, or resources can you invest for the sake of the kingdom of God, even if you have no guarantee of success?

_____

_____

_____

_____

_____

_____

_____

_____

_____

_____

_____

_____

SPIRITUAL GOALS FOR THE WEEK

_____

_____

_____

_____

_____

_____

_____

_____

_____

_____

_____

_____

GOLDEN MERCIES

---- 19 ----

"Peace I leave with you, My peace I give to you; not as the world gives
do I give to you. Let not your heart be troubled, neither let it be afraid."
JOHN 14:27

*D*id you ever hear of a man who gave a beggar something to encourage him to keep on begging of you? I must confess I never did such a thing, and am not likely to begin. But that is just what Christ does. When he gives us a little grace, his motive is to make us ask for more; and when he gives us more grace, it is given with the very motive to make us come and ask again. He gives us silver blessings to induce us to ask for golden mercies; and when we have golden favors, those same mercies are given on purpose to lead us to pray more earnestly, and open our mouth wider, that we may receive more. What a strange giver Christ is! What a strange friend, that he gives on purpose to make us beg more!

The more you ask of Christ, the more you can ask; the more you have got, the more you will want; the more you know Him, the more you will desire to know Him; the more grace you receive, the more grace you will pant after; and when you are full of grace, you will never be content till you get full of glory. Christ's way of giving is, "Of his fullness we have all received, and grace for grace"—grace to make us pant for grace; grace to make us long after something higher, something fuller and richer still. "I do not give to you as the world gives."

RESPONDING IN PRAYER

"Lord, please whet my appetite for more by granting
my requests according to Your will. Through realizing
Your desire to give, help me to pray more fervently."

Continuing in prayer . . .

_____

_____

_____

_____

_____

FOR REFLECTION

What answers to prayer have caused you to have even greater faith, seeking God for more and greater things? Did He answer your prayer?

_____
_____
_____
_____
_____
_____
_____
_____
_____
_____

SPIRITUAL GOALS FOR THE WEEK

_____
_____
_____
_____
_____
_____
_____
_____

TO BE WITH CHRIST

---- 20 ----

I am hard pressed between the two, having a desire
to depart and be with Christ, which is far better.
PHILIPPIANS 1:23

*T*hat you are as yet a babe in grace is clear from your admission that to depart and be with Christ does not seem to be a better thing for you than to abide in the flesh.

Should it not be the business of this life to prepare for the next life, and, in that respect, to prepare to die? But how can a man be prepared for that which he never thinks of? Do you mean to take a leap in the dark? If so, you are in an unhappy condition, and I beseech you as you love your own soul to escape from such peril by the help of God's Holy Spirit.

"Oh," says one, "but I do not feel called upon to think of it." Why, the very autumn of the year calls you to it. Each fading leaf admonishes you. You will most surely have to die; why not think upon the inevitable? It is said that the ostrich buries its head in the sand and fancies itself secure when it can no longer see the hunter. I can hardly fancy that even a bird can be quite so foolish, and I beseech you do not enact such madness. If I do not think of death, yet death will think of me. If I will not go to death by meditation and consideration, death will come to me. Let me, then, meet it like a man, and to that end let me look it in the face.

RESPONDING IN PRAYER

"Lord, take away my fear of death, knowing that You
are Lord of the entire process, so that I will not cling to
the things of this earth but look forward to Your eternal presence."

Continuing in prayer . . .

_____

_____

_____

_____

_____

Write about any fears you may have of death. Then pray about how God is in charge of the process and how He has dealt with death through Christ.

_____

_____

_____

_____

_____

_____

_____

_____

_____

_____

_____

SPIRITUAL GOALS FOR THE WEEK

_____

_____

_____

_____

_____

_____

_____

_____

_____

FAMILIAR WITH SIN

—— 21 ——

Has then what is good become death to me? Certainly not! But sin,
that it might appear sin, was producing death in me through what is good,
so that sin through the commandment might become exceedingly sinful.
ROMANS 7:13

*B*y degrees men get familiar with sin. The ear in which the cannon has been booming will not notice slight sounds. At first a little sin startles us; but soon we say, "Is it not a little one?" Then there comes another, larger, and then another, until by degrees we begin to regard sin as but a little ill; and then follows an unholy presumption: "We have not fallen into open sin. True, we tripped a little, but we stood upright in the main. We may have uttered one unholy word, but as for the most of our conversation, it has been consistent." So we palliate sin; we throw a cloak over it; we call it by dainty names.

Christian, beware how you think lightly of sin. Take heed lest you fall by little and little. Sin, a *little* thing? Is it not a poison? Who knows its deadliness? Sin, a little thing? Do not the little foxes spoil the grapes? Does not the tiny coral insect build a rock which wrecks a navy? Do not little strokes fell lofty oaks? Will not continual droppings wear away stones?

Sin, a little thing? It girded the Redeemer's head with thorns, and pierced His heart! It made *Him* suffer anguish, bitterness, and woe. Could you weigh the least sin in the scales of eternity, you would fly from it as from a serpent, and abhor the least appearance of evil.

RESPONDING IN PRAYER

"Lord, I know that sin cannot be tolerated in my life so help me
wage an unceasing battle against all sin in my life with Your help."

Continuing in prayer . . .

_____

_____

_____

_____

_____

When has your conscience been desensitized through the tolerance of small sins over a period of time? What can you do to change and allow for the Holy Spirit's conviction?

_____

_____

_____

_____

_____

_____

_____

_____

_____

_____

SPIRITUAL GOALS FOR THE WEEK

_____

_____

_____

_____

_____

_____

_____

_____

_____

_____

THE GLORIOUS HOPE

───── 22 ─────

"Watch therefore, for you do not know what hour your Lord is coming."
MATTHEW 24:42

*H*e will come; but when He comes, no spirit in heaven or on earth should pretend to know. Oh, it is my joyous hope that He may come while yet I live! Perhaps there may be some of us here who shall be alive and remain at the coming of the Son of man. Oh, glorious hope! We shall have to sleep, but we shall all be changed. He may come now, and we that are alive and remain shall be forever with Him. But if you die, Christian, this is your hope. "I will come again and receive you to Myself; that where I am, there you may be also." And this is to be your duty, "Watch, therefore, for you do not know what hour your Lord is coming."

Oh, will I not work on for Christ is at the door! Oh, I will not give up toiling never so hard for my Master comes, and His reward is with Him, and His work before Him, giving unto every man according as his work shall be. Oh, I will not lie down in despair, for the trump is sounding now. Methinks I hear the trampling of the conquering legion; the last of God's mighty heroes are even now, perhaps, born into the world. The hour of this revival is the hour of turning to the battle; thick has been the fight and hot and furious the struggle, but the trump of the conqueror is beginning to sound, the angel is lifting it now to his lips.

He comes, He comes, and every eye shall see Him, and they that have crucified Him shall weep and wail before Him, but the righteous shall rejoice and shall magnify Him exceedingly.

RESPONDING IN PRAYER

*"Lord, though I do not know when You are returning to this earth,
let me hope expectantly and be willing to fight the good fight of faith,
knowing victory is mine because He has won the battles."*

Continuing in prayer . . .

_____

_____

_____

_____

_____

What battles or causes should I be involved in, knowing that Jesus will one day return and what I have done for His cause will have an effect throughout eternity?

_____

_____

_____

_____

_____

_____

_____

_____

_____

_____

SPIRITUAL GOALS FOR THE WEEK

_____

_____

_____

_____

_____

_____

_____

_____

_____

A LIVING UNION

───┤23├───

"I am the vine; you are the branches. He who abides in Me and I in him,
bears much fruit; for without Me you can do nothing."
JOHN 15:5

*W*e must bear fruit, or we shall certainly perish; and we cannot have fruit unless we have Christ. We must be knit to Christ, vitally one with Him, just as a branch is really, after a living fashion, one with the stem. It would be no use to tie a branch to the stem of the vine; that would not cause it to bring forth fruit. It must be joined to it in a living union. So must you and I be livingly joined to Christ. Do you know, by experience, what that expression means? For, if you do not know it by experience, you do not know it at all. No man knows what life is but the one who is himself alive, and no man knows what union to Christ is but he who is himself united to Christ.

We must become one with Christ by an act of faith; we must be inserted into Him as the graft is placed in the incision made in the tree into which it is to be grafted. Then there must be a knitting of the two together, a vital junction, a union of life, and a flowing of the sap, or else there cannot be any bearing of fruit. Again, I say, what a serious thing this makes our life to be! Our earnest should be our questioning of ourselves!

RESPONDING IN PRAYER

"Lord, help me to know by experience what a living union
with You really means and how I might bear fruit that is
a proof of my salvation and a way to bring glory to You."

Continuing in prayer . . .

_____

_____

_____

_____

_____

FOR REFLECTION

Name what you consider to be spiritual fruit in your church, family, and work life within the last year.

_____

_____

_____

_____

_____

_____

_____

_____

_____

_____

SPIRITUAL GOALS FOR THE WEEK

_____

_____

_____

_____

_____

_____

_____

_____

_____

_____

_____

DON'T HOLD BACK

24

In whom we have boldness and
access with confidence through faith in Him.
EPHESIANS 3:12

You are invited, nay, you are commanded to pray; come therefore with boldness to the throne of grace. Dear friend, are you already saved? Then *keep not back* from union with the Lord's people. Neglect not the ordinances of baptism and the Lord's Supper. You may be of a timid disposition, but you must strive against it, lest it lead you into disobedience. There is a sweet promise made to those who confess Christ—by no means miss it, lest you come under the condemnation of those who deny Him.

If you have talents, *keep not back* from using them. Hoard not your wealth, waste not your time; let not your abilities rust or your influence be unused. Jesus kept not back, imitate Him by being foremost in self-denials and self-sacrifices.

Keep not back from close communion with God, from boldly appropriating covenant blessings, from advancing in the divine life, from prying into the precious mysteries of the love of Christ. Neither, beloved friend, be guilty of keeping others back by your coldness, harshness, or suspicions. For Jesus' sake, go forward yourself, and encourage others to do the like. Hell and the leaguered bands of superstition and infidelity are forward to the fight. Oh, soldiers of the cross, keep not back.

RESPONDING IN PRAYER

"Lord, may all my thoughts, words, and actions have the
awareness of heaven and the presence of Jesus close by.
Help me to meditate more often on the things of Christ."

Continuing in prayer . . .

_____

_____

_____

_____

_____

FOR REFLECTION

When have you taken it for granted that you were standing in Christ and then
fell because you were not actively following Him?

_____

_____

_____

_____

_____

_____

_____

_____

_____

SPIRITUAL GOALS FOR THE WEEK

_____

_____

_____

_____

_____

_____

_____

_____

_____

THE WORLD'S TWILIGHT

25

"I saw in the night visions, and behold, a fourth beast,
dreadful and terrible, exceedingly strong. . . It was devouring,
breaking in pieces, and trampling the residue with its feet."

DANIEL 7:7

We may expect to see darker evening times than have ever been beheld. Let us not imagine that our civilization shall be more enduring than any other that has gone before it, unless the Lord shall preserve it. It may be that the suggestion will be realized which has often been laughed at as folly, that one day men should sit upon the broken arches of London Bridge, and marvel at the civilization that has departed, just as men walk over the mounds of Nimrod, and marvel at cities buried there. It is just possible that all the civilization of this country may die out in blackest night; it may be that God will repeat again the great story: "I saw in the night visions, and behold, a fourth beast, dreadful and terrible, exceedingly strong. . . It was devouring, breaking in pieces, and trampling the residue with its feet."

But if ever such things should be—if the world should be—if the world should ever have to return to barbarism and darkness—if instead of what we sometimes hope for, a constant progress to the brightest day, all of our hopes should be blasted, let us rest quite satisfied that "at evening time . . . it will be light" (Zechariah 14:7), that the end of the world's history shall be an end of glory. However red with blood, however black with sin the world may yet be, she shall one day be as pure and perfect as when she was created.

RESPONDING IN PRAYER

"Lord, we live in dark times and can clearly see the
emptiness of human progress. Help me not to be discouraged
knowing that at the end You will restore all things."

Continuing in prayer . . .

Where in your own life have you fallen for the myth of human progress? Have you pinned your hopes and security on earthly things rather than the coming kingdom?

_____

_____

_____

_____

_____

_____

_____

_____

_____

_____

SPIRITUAL GOALS FOR THE WEEK

_____

_____

_____

_____

_____

_____

_____

_____

_____

TRUE RELIGION

26

Oh, taste and see that the Lord is good;
blessed is the man who trusts in Him!

PSALM 34:8

*S*ome men say that they will test the holiness of Christ's religion by the holiness of Christ's people. You have no right, I reply, to put the question to any such test as that. The proper test that you ought to use is to try it yourselves—to "taste and see that the Lord is good." By tasting and seeing you will prove His goodness, and by the same process you must prove the holiness of His Gospel. Your business is to seek Christ crucified for yourselves, not to take the representation of another man concerning the power of grace to subdue corruption and to sanctify the heart.

Inasmuch as God has given you a Bible, He intended you to read it and not to be content with reading *men*. You are not to be content with feelings that rise through the conversation of others; your only power to know true religion is by having His Holy Spirit operating upon your own heart that you may yourself experience what is the power of religion. You have no right to judge religion from anything extra or external from itself. And if you despise it before you have tried it yourself, you must stand confessed in this world as a fool, and in the next world as a criminal. And yet this is so with most men. If you hear a man rail at the Bible, you may usually conclude that he never reads it.

RESPONDING IN PRAYER

"Lord, help me not to judge Your truth based upon what I see
in others but upon Your holy Word and the work done
in my own heart by the Holy Spirit."

Continuing in prayer . . .

Has your faith been negatively affected by some failure on the part of humans? Give this to God and confess that only He is perfect.

_____

_____

_____

_____

_____

_____

_____

_____

_____

_____

SPIRITUAL GOALS FOR THE WEEK

_____

_____

_____

_____

_____

_____

_____

_____

_____

JUSTIFIED SINNERS

27

But now, thus says the Lord, who created you, O Jacob,
and He who formed you, O Israel: "Fear not, for I have redeemed you;
I have called you by your name; you are Mine."

ISAIAH 43:1

*W*hen we cannot see our way, or cannot make out what to do, we need not be at all troubled concerning it, for the Lord Jehovah can see a way out of every intricacy. There never was a problem so hard to solve as that which is answered in redemption. Herein was the tremendous difficulty: How can God be just, and yet be the Savior of sinners? How can He fulfill His threatenings, and yet forgive sin? If that problem had been left to angels and men, they could never have worked it out throughout eternity; but God has solved it through freely delivering up His own Son. In the glorious sacrifice of Jesus we see the justice of God magnified, for He laid sin on the blessed Lord, who had become one with His chosen.

Jesus identified Himself with His people, and therefore their sin was laid upon Him, and the sword of the Lord awoke against Him. He was not taken arbitrarily to be a victim, but He was a voluntary sufferer. His relationship amounted to covenant oneness with His people, and "it was necessary for the Christ to suffer." Herein is a wisdom which must be more than equal to all minor perplexities.

Hear this, then, O poor soul in suspense! Let us commit our way unto the Lord. Mine is a peculiarly difficult one, but I know that my Redeemer lives, and He will lead me by a right way. He will be our Guide even unto death; and after death He will guide us through those tracks unknown of the mysterious region and cause us to rest with Him forever.

RESPONDING IN PRAYER

"Lord, Your justice is magnified in causing Jesus to
become sin for us, but so is Your mercy. Thank You that
You can justify me even though I still sin."

Continuing in prayer . . .

_____

_____

_____

FOR REFLECTION

Give examples as to how Jesus has become your guide through difficult places in
life. Write down ways in which you would like guidance now.

_____

_____

_____

_____

_____

_____

_____

_____

_____

_____

SPIRITUAL GOALS FOR THE WEEK

_____

_____

_____

_____

_____

_____

_____

_____

THE BREAD OF LIFE

| 28 |

And when I saw Him, I fell at His feet as dead.

REVELATION 1:17

When we see Jesus, our Savior, the Savior of sinners, surely self will sink, and humility will fall at His feet. When we think of Gethsemane and Calvary, and all our great Redeemer's pain and agony, surely, by the Holy Ghost, self-glorying, self-seeking, and self-will must fall as though slain with a deadly wound. "When I saw Him, I fell at His feet as dead" (Revelation 1:17).

Jesus has placed upon this table food. The bread sets forth all that is necessary, and the cup all that is luxurious: provision for all our wants and for all our right desires, all that we need for sustenance and joy. Then what a poverty-stricken soul am I that I cannot find myself in bread! As to comforts, I may not think of them; they must be given me or I shall never taste them. Brothers, we are gentlemen commoners upon the bounty of our great Kinsman: we come to His table for our maintenance, we have no establishments of our own. He who feeds the sparrows feeds our souls; in spiritual things we no more gather into barns than do the blessed birds; our heavenly Father feeds us from that "all fullness" which it has pleased Him to lay up for us in Jesus.

We could not live an hour spiritually without Him who is not only bread, but life; not only the wine which cheers, but consolation itself. Our life hangs upon Jesus; He is our Head as well as our food. We shall never outgrow our need of natural bread, and, spiritually, we shall never rise out of our need of a present Christ, but rather we shall feel a stronger craving and a more urgent passion for Him.

RESPONDING IN PRAYER

"Lord, let me approach the table of the Lord's Supper
with reverence and thanksgiving, knowing that
You feed my soul in a special way at Your table and
I come away with a new appreciation for the sacrifice at Calvary."

Continuing in prayer . . .

Write out the most significant factors regarding the Lord's Supper that edify you. How can you receive more from this grace-filled experience in the future?

_____

_____

_____

_____

_____

_____

_____

_____

_____

_____

_____

SPIRITUAL GOALS FOR THE WEEK

_____

_____

_____

_____

_____

_____

_____

_____

_____

_____

_____

_____

LARGE ANSWERS TO PRAYER

---29---

I am the Lord your God, who brought you out of the land of Egypt;
open your mouth wide, and I will fill it.

PSALM 81:10

*C*hristians should elevate the scale of their praying and enlarge their requests, and never let it be said that they lose blessings solely by failing to ask for them. Dear brothers and sisters, we may well ask great things, for we are asking of *a great God,* who fills immensity, who has all power, who has all blessings in His stores. If we were to ask Him for a world, it is no more for Him to bestow a world than it would be for us to give away a crumb.

When the poor widow gave her two mites she gave her all, and knowing her poverty one would ask very little of her, and expect even less; but when you ask a king you do not expect two mites from him. That poor woman who said, "True, Lord, yet even the dogs eat of the crumbs that fall from their master's table," was far nearer the mark than most of us, for much as she valued the inestimable blessing which she sought, she reckoned it as being nothing more than a crumb as it came from God.

The greatest blessings which can yet be received through Jesus Christ, though we cannot prize them enough, and they are beyond all calculation precious, are little in comparison with the unspeakable gift of His Son, which has already been bestowed. Open your mouth wide, for wide are the supplies of love, and boundless the riches of the sovereign grace of so great a God.

RESPONDING IN PRAYER

"Lord, enlarge my faith so that I can ask for bigger things
according to Your will, and not be afraid to recognize
that You are a great and mighty God."

Continuing in prayer . . .

_____

_____

_____

_____

Give God a list of your prayers that you feel require the greatest faith on your part. Make sure they are requests that will bring Him greater glory.

_____

_____

_____

_____

_____

_____

_____

_____

_____

_____

SPIRITUAL GOALS FOR THE WEEK

_____

_____

_____

_____

_____

_____

_____

_____

_____

PRAYERS DURING PROSPERITY

───────── 30 ─────────

"And all things, whatever you ask in prayer,
believing, you will receive."
MATTHEW 21:22

ℋow infrequent and few are your prayers, and yet how numerous and how great have God's blessings been. You have prayed in times of difficulty very earnestly, but when God has delivered you, where was your former fervency? In the day of trouble you besieged His throne with all your might and in the hour of your prosperity, you could not wholly cease from supplication, but oh, how faint was the prayer compared with that which was wrung out of your soul by the rough hand of your agony. Yet, notwithstanding that, though you have ceased to pray as you once did, God has not ceased to bless.

Oh! I marvel that the Lord should regard those intermittent spasms of importunity which come and go with our necessities. Oh! What a God is He that He should hear the prayers of men who come to Him when they have wants, but who neglect Him when they have received a mercy, who approach Him when they are forced to come, but who almost forget to go to Him when mercies are plentiful and sorrows are few. Look at your prayers, again, in another aspect. *How unbelieving have they often been!* You and I have gone to the mercy seat, and we have asked God to bless us, but we have not believed that He would do so.

He has said, "If you believe, you will receive whatever you ask for in prayer." Oh! how I could smite myself when I think how on my knees I have doubted my God!

RESPONDING IN PRAYER

"Lord, help me to pray as earnestly during the good times in
my life as during the bad. Give me a holy fear of missing out
on Your blessings because I feel content and independent."

Continuing in prayer . . .

_____

_____

_____

_____

FOR REFLECTION

Review your cycles of praying during your Christian life. How often have you been thankful and worshipped when God has answered your needs versus your prayers during times of need or trial?

_____

_____

_____

_____

_____

_____

_____

_____

_____

_____

SPIRITUAL GOALS FOR THE WEEK

_____

_____

_____

_____

_____

_____

_____

_____

GUARD YOUR HEART

─────────────────┤ 31 ├─────────────────

Keep your heart with all diligence, for out of it spring the issues of life.
PROVERBS 4:23

*W*hen a man becomes cold, indifferent, and careless, one of the first things that will suffer will be his devotion. When a sick man is in a decline, his lungs suffer and his voice; and so when a Christian is in a spiritual decline, the breath of prayer is affected, and the cry of supplication becomes weak. Prayer is the true gauge of spiritual power. To restrain prayer is dangerous and of deadly tendency.

You may depend upon it that what you are upon your knees you are really before your God. What the Pharisee and the publican were in prayer was the true criterion of their spiritual state. You may maintain a decent repute among men, but it is a small matter to be judged of man's judgment, for men see only the surface, while the Lord's eyes pry into the recesses of the soul. If He sees that you are prayerless, He makes small account of your attendance at religious meetings or your loud professions of conversion.

If you are a man of earnest prayer, and especially if the spirit of prayer be in you, so that in addition to certain seasons of supplication your heart habitually talks with God, things are right with you; but if this be not the case, and your prayers be "hindered," there is something in your spiritual system which needs to be ejected, or somewhat lacking which ought at once to be supplied. "Above all else, guard your heart, for it is the wellspring of life."

RESPONDING IN PRAYER

"Lord, help me to continually take my spiritual temperature and reveal to me any signs of coldness, indifference, or carelessness. Show me both what needs to be discarded as well as supplied in my prayer life."

Continuing in prayer . . .

_____

_____

_____

_____

_____

FOR REFLECTION

How much of a role does prayer play in your overall walk with the Lord? Ask
God how He measures you by what you are on your knees for.

_____

_____

_____

_____

_____

_____

_____

_____

_____

SPIRITUAL GOALS FOR THE WEEK

_____

_____

_____

_____

_____

_____

_____

_____

_____

_____

RECONCILED TO GOD

———————— 32 ————————

Moses and Aaron were among His priests, and Samuel was among those who called upon His name; they called upon the Lord, and He answered them.

PSALM 99:6

The Lord will hear any man's prayer who asks for mercy through the mediation of the Lord Jesus. He never despises the cry of the contrite. He is a God ready to hear all those who seek reconciliation; but concerning other matters it is true that God heareth not sinners—that is, while they remain sinners He will not grant them their wishes—indeed, to do so would encourage them in their sins. If they will repent and cry for mercy through Jesus Christ He will hear their cry, and will save them; but if they are not first reconciled to Him, their prayers are empty wind.

A man will grant his child's request, but he does not listen to strangers; he will listen to his friends, but not to enemies. It is not fit that the golden key which opens the caskets of heaven should be hung at a rebel's girdle. Yet more, God does not hear all His children alike, or alike at all times. It is not every believer who is mighty in prayer. Read the ninety-ninth Psalm, and you will find words like these: "Moses and Aaron were among His priests, and Samuel was among those who called on His name; they called upon the Lord, and He answered them." Yes; he answered *them*—Moses, Aaron, Samuel—he answered them, for they kept His testimonies.

When children of God find that their prayers do not succeed, they should search, and they would soon discover a reason why their prayers are hindered.

RESPONDING IN PRAYER

"Lord, I am so grateful that You never reject my prayer when I am humble and sincere. Please reconcile me in all areas of my life so that I might become a mighty prayer warrior."

Continuing in prayer . . .

_____

_____

_____

Do you see the relationship between keeping God's commands and answered prayers in the lives of Moses, Aaron, and Samuel? What about in your own life?

_____

_____

_____

_____

_____

_____

_____

_____

_____

SPIRITUAL GOALS FOR THE WEEK

_____

_____

_____

_____

_____

_____

_____

_____

A PLEDGE OF THE SPIRIT

33

"If you then, being evil, know how to give good gifts
to your children, how much more will your heavenly Father
give the Holy Spirit to those who ask Him!"
LUKE 11:13

*D*id you ever hear of a man who when his child asked for bread gave him a stone? Go to the worst part of London, and will you find a man of that kind? You shall, if you like, get among pirates and murderers, and when a little child cries, "Father, give me a bit of bread and meat," does the most wicked father fill his own little one's mouth with stones? Yet the Lord seems to say that this is what He would be doing if He were to deny us the Holy Spirit when we ask Him for his necessary working: He would be like one that gave his children stones instead of bread.

Do you think the Lord will ever bring Himself down to that? But he says, "*How much more* shall your heavenly Father give the Holy Spirit to those that ask Him?" He makes it a stronger case than that of an ordinary parent. The Lord must give us the Spirit when we ask Him, for He has herein bound Himself by no ordinary pledge. He has used a simile which would bring dishonor on His own name, and that of the very grossest kind, if He did not give the Holy Spirit to those that ask Him.

Oh, then, let us ask Him at once, with all our hearts. Am I not so happy as to have in this audience some who will immediately ask? I pray that some who have never received the Holy Spirit at all may now be led, while I am speaking, to pray, "Blessed Spirit, visit me; lead me to Jesus." But especially those of you that are the children of God, to you is this promise especially made. Ask God to make you all that the Spirit of God can make you, not only a satisfied believer who has drunk for himself, but a useful believer, who overflows the neighborhood with blessing.

RESPONDING IN PRAYER

"Lord, I pray that You will give me the Holy Spirit in
abundance in order to know Jesus better and to have
the power to live a life that will draw others to You."

Continuing in prayer . . .

FOR REFLECTION

To what degree do you include the Holy Spirit in your plans to serve God? Ask the Father to pour out His Spirit and to bring to remembrance your need for Him.

_____

_____

_____

_____

_____

_____

_____

_____

_____

SPIRITUAL GOALS FOR THE WEEK

_____

_____

_____

_____

_____

_____

_____

_____

_____

CHRIST IN YOU

---- 34 ----

"For God so loved the world that He gave His only begotten Son, that whoever believes in him should not perish but have everlasting life."

JOHN 3:16

*Z*he struggle becomes more and more intense; each victory over sin reveals another army of evil tendencies, and I am never able to sheathe my sword, nor cease from prayer and watchfulness. I cannot advance an inch without praying my way, nor keep the inch I gain without watching and standing fast. Grace alone can preserve and perfect me.

The old nature will kill the new nature if it can; and to this moment the only reason why my new nature is not dead is this—because it cannot die. If it could have died, it would have been slain long ago; but Jesus said, "He who believes in Me has everlasting life" (John 6:47); and therefore the believer cannot die. The only religion which will save you is one that you cannot leave, because it possesses you, and will not leave you. To have Christ living in you, and the truth ingrained in your very nature—O sirs, *this* is the thing that saves the soul, and nothing short of it.

It is written in the text, "For God so loved the world that he gave His only begotten Son, that whoever believes in him should not perish but have everlasting life." What is this but a life that shall last through your three-score years and ten; a life that will outshine those stars and yon sun and moon; a life that shall remain with the life of the Eternal Father? As long as there is a God, the believer shall not only exist, but live.

RESPONDING IN PRAYER

"Lord, I do not want to merely exist but to live the fullness of life that is implied with Your description of everlasting life. May that life never leave me."

Continuing in prayer . . .

_____

_____

_____

_____

What are the particular weaknesses of your old nature that war against your new nature? Seek God for greater wisdom and grace in learning to deal with them.

_____

_____

_____

_____

_____

_____

_____

_____

_____

_____

_____

SPIRITUAL GOALS FOR THE WEEK

_____

_____

_____

_____

_____

_____

_____

_____

_____

_____

GODLY SORROW

───┤35├───

Or do you despise the riches of His goodness, forbearance, and longsuffering,
not knowing that the goodness of God leads you to repentance?
ROMANS 2:4

*W*hen a man is tied up to be flogged for a deed of brutal violence, and his back is bared for the last, depend upon it that he repents of what he did; that is to say, he repents that he has to suffer for it; but that is all, and a sorry all too. He has no sorrow for the agony which he inflicted on his innocent victim; no regret for maiming him for life. What is the value of such a repentance? Here is the point: do you wish to have new hearts? If you do, you shall have them. Do you wish to leave the sins you have loved? Do you desire to live as Christ lived? Do you wish to keep the commandments to be as God would have you to be, just, loving, kind, chaste, after the example of the great Redeemer?

If so, then truly the desire you have comes from God; but if all you want is to be able to die without dread, that you may wake up in the next world and not be driven down to the bottomless pit—if that is all, there is nothing gracious in it, and it is no wonder that you should say, "The harvest is past, the summer is ended, and I am not saved." You do not know what being saved means.

God teach you to love holiness, and there shall not pass another harvest, nay not another day, before you shall be saved; indeed, that very love is the dawn of salvation. Seek salvation as the kingdom of God within you, seek it first and seek it now, and you shall not be denied.

RESPONDING IN PRAYER

"Lord, I pray that the sorrow for my sins may not stem from fear of punishment as much as from a love based on a fear of offending You."

Continuing in prayer . . .

_____

_____

_____

_____

_____

_____

What does loving holiness mean in terms of your senses? That is, how will the desire for holiness affect what you see, what you hear, and what you speak?

_____

_____

_____

_____

_____

_____

_____

_____

_____

_____

SPIRITUAL GOALS FOR THE WEEK

_____

_____

_____

_____

_____

_____

_____

_____

_____

THE BEAUTY OF HOLINESS

---| 36 |---

Let the beauty of the Lord our God be upon us;
Yes, establish the work of our hands.

PSALMS 90:17

*L*et the beauty of the Lord our God be upon us." Sorrow mars the countenance and clothes the body with sackcloth; but if the Lord will come to us and adorn us with His beauty, then the stains of mourning will speedily disappear. What a beauty is this which the Lord gives—"the beauty of the Lord our God!" This comeliness is the beauty of His grace; for our covenant God is the God of all grace. If the Lord makes us to know that we are His, our faces shine. If He fills us with His life and love, then brightness flashes from the eyes, and there is a grace about every movement.

This "beauty" means holiness; for holiness is the beauty of God. If the Holy Spirit works in you the beauty of holiness, you will rise superior to your afflictions. If this church shall be made the holier by its bereavements, we shall gain much by our losses. This beauty of the Lord must surely mean His presence with us. As the sun beautifies all things, so does God's presence. When we know that Jesus is with us, when we feel that He is our Helper, when we bask in His love, when He abides with us in power, this is the beauty of the saints. If we have Christ in us, Christ with us, we can bear any amount of trouble.

This beauty gives to the believer an attractiveness in the eyes of men: they perceive that we have been with Jesus, and they behold our faces shining like the faces of angels. It is a great thing when a Christian is so happy, so holy, and so heavenly that he attracts others to Christ, and people seek his company because they perceive that he has been in the company of the blessed Lord.

RESPONDING IN PRAYER

"Lord, sometimes I think of Your holiness as being forbidding rather than beautiful. Give me the capacity to take in and worship Your beauty and thus be drawn in a greater way to Your holiness."

Continuing in prayer . . .

FOR REFLECTION

What Scripture passages or lines from great Christian writers inspire you in the areas of God's beauty and majesty? How would you describe your own encounters?

_____

_____

_____

_____

_____

_____

_____

_____

_____

_____

SPIRITUAL GOALS FOR THE WEEK

_____

_____

_____

_____

_____

_____

_____

_____

STONES THAT SPEAK

You also, as living stones, are being built up a spiritual house,
a holy priesthood, to offer up spiritual sacrifices
acceptable to God through Jesus Christ.

1 PETER 2:5

If the stones were to speak they could tell of their Maker; and shall not we tell of Him who made us anew, and out of stones raised up children unto Abraham? They could speak of ages long since gone; the old rocks could tell of chaos and order, and the handiwork of God in various stages of creation's drama; and cannot we talk of God's decrees, of God's great work in ancient times, and all that He did for His church? If the stones were to speak they could tell of their breaker, how He took them from the quarry, and made them fit for the temple; and cannot we tell of our Creator and Maker, who broke our hearts with the hammer of His word that He might build us into His temple? If the stones were to speak, they would tell of their Builder, who polished them and fashioned them after the similitude of a palace; and shall not we talk of our Architect and Builder, who has put us in our place in the temple of the living God?

Oh, if the stones could speak, they might have a long, long story to tell by way of memorial, for many a time hath a great stone been rolled as a memorial unto God; and we can tell of Ebenezers—stones of help, stones of remembrance. The broken stones of the Law cry out against us, but Christ Himself, who has rolled away the stone from the door of the sepulchre, speaks for us.

Stones might well cry out, but we will not let them: we will hush their noise with ours, we will break forth into sacred song, and bless the majesty of the Most High all our days.

RESPONDING IN PRAYER

"Lord, I am in wonder at all You have built in Your creation,
in Your laws, and most of all in what You have done in me through
the work of Jesus Christ. May I be a living temple to Your glory."

Continuing in prayer . . .

If you were to create five piles of stones as a memorial to the chief works of God in your life, how would you describe each one?

_____

_____

_____

_____

_____

_____

_____

_____

_____

_____

SPIRITUAL GOALS FOR THE WEEK

_____

_____

_____

_____

_____

_____

_____

_____

_____

_____

WHILE IT IS DAY

---38---

*But take heed to yourselves, lest your hearts be weighed
down with carousing, drunkenness and cares of this life,
and that Day come on you unexpectedly.*

LUKE 21:34

You have come from your house tonight, and you have left at home a dear friend to whom you wish to speak about his soul. Do it tonight, for he may die in the night. I think I read it in the life of Dr. Chalmers, that on one occasion he spent an evening with a number of friends, and there was present a Highland chieftain, a very interesting character. They spent the evening in telling anecdotes of their lives, and repeating extracts from various entertaining works of voyages and travels—spent the evening, as we should think, very properly indeed, and after having very much enjoyed themselves, they went to bed.

At midnight, the whole family were startled from their sleep, for the Highland chieftain was in the pangs and agonies of death. He went up to his chamber in sound health, but died in the night. The impression upon Chalmers' mind was this: "Had I known that he would have so died, would not the evening have been differently spent? Then ought it not to have been spent in a very different manner by men all of whom might have died?" He felt as if the blood of that man's soul in some measure fell upon him; the occurrence itself was a lasting blessing to him.

May it be so to us in the hearing of the story, and from this time forth may we work with all our might "while it is day."

RESPONDING IN PRAYER

*"Lord, please do not let me miss any opportunities to
share the salvation message with those who do not know You,
for it may be the last chance for them to hear, accept Your forgiveness,
and be saved from eternal punishment."*

Continuing in prayer . . .

_____

_____

_____

Pray about three people that may hear the Gospel for the first time. Ask God to give you the right opportunity to at least plant seeds in their lives.

_____

_____

_____

_____

_____

_____

_____

_____

_____

SPIRITUAL GOALS FOR THE WEEK

_____

_____

_____

_____

_____

_____

_____

_____

THE THRONE OF YOUR HEART

39

Blessed be the God and Father of our Lord Jesus Christ,
the Father of mercies and God of all comfort.
2 CORINTHIANS 1:3

*N*one of your dearest and most cherished loves is at all worthy to sit upon the throne of your heart. Far down in the scale must they be placed when the God who gave them to you is brought into comparison. That broad bosom of your beloved husband beats fondly and faithfully, but when death lays it low, as ere long it must, how wretched will be your condition if you have not an everlasting Comforter upon whose breast to lean! Those dear little sparkling eyes, which are like stars in the heaven of your social joy, if these be the gods of your idolatry, how wretched will be your condition if you have not an everlasting Comforter upon whose breast to lean! Those dear little sparkling eyes, which are like stars in the heaven of your social joy, if these be the gods of your idolatry, how wretched will you be when their brightness is dim, and the mother's joy is moldering back to dust!

Happy is the one who has an everlasting joy and an undying comfort; and there is none in this respect like unto the God of Jeshurun. There would be fewer broken hearts if hearts were more completely the Lord's. We should have no rebellious spirits if, when we had our joys, we used them lawfully, and did not too much build our hopes upon them. All beneath the moon will wane. Everything on these shores ebbs and flows like the sea. Everything beneath the sun will be eclipsed. You will not find in time that which is only to be discovered in eternity, namely, an immutable and unfailing source of comfort.

RESPONDING IN PRAYER

"Lord, I know that everything in this life will pass away
on this earth. Help me to take comfort in eternal realities,
first and foremost being Yourself."

Continuing in prayer . . .

_____

_____

_____

_____

What earthly things are on the throne of your heart in place of God? Ask God how you can understand deep within your soul that He is more satisfying than the things you listed.

_____

_____

_____

_____

_____

_____

_____

_____

_____

SPIRITUAL GOALS FOR THE WEEK

_____

_____

_____

_____

_____

_____

_____

_____

BROKEN ARROWS

40

He teaches my hands to make war,
so that my arms can bend a bow of bronze.

PSALM 18:34

I think I see before me the hero of Golgotha using His cross as an anvil, and his woes as a hammer, and dashing to slivers bundle after bundle of our sins, those poisoned "arrows of the bow;" trampling on every charge, and destroying every accusation. What glorious blows the mighty breaker gives! How the weapons fly to fragments, beaten small as the dust of the threshing floor! Behold, I see Him drawing from its sheath of hellish workmanship the dread sword of hellish power! See, He shapes it across His knee, as a man breaks the dry wood of a fagot, and casts it into the fire.

Like David, He cries, "He teaches my hands to make war, my arms can bend a bow of bronze." "I have pursued my enemies and overtook them; Neither did I turn back again till they were destroyed. And I have destroyed them . . . so that they could not rise; they have fallen under my feet. . . . I beat them as fine as dust borne on the wind; I poured them out like mud in the streets" (2 Samuel 22:38–39, 43).

Beloved, no sin of a believer can now be an arrow mortally to wound Him, no condemnation can now be a sword to kill Him, for the punishment of our sin was borne by Christ. A full atonement has been made for all our iniquities by our blessed Substitute and Surety. Who now accuses? Who now condemns? Christ has died, yea, rather He has risen again. Let hell, if it can, find a single arrow to shoot against the beloved of the Lord. They are all broken; not one of them is left.

RESPONDING IN PRAYER

"Lord, what a wonderful thought that no weapons of the world,
the flesh, or the devil can ever harm me. Help me to put on
the full armor of God for protection in spiritual battle."

Continuing in prayer . . .

_____

_____

_____

_____

When have darts or arrows wounded you temporarily because you were not walking with the Lord and covered with the protection of His Spirit? Ask God how you can better be ready next time.

_____

_____

_____

_____

_____

_____

_____

_____

_____

SPIRITUAL GOALS FOR THE WEEK

_____

_____

_____

_____

_____

_____

_____

THE JEALOUSY OF GOD

─────│41│─────

You shall worship no other god, for the Lord,
whose name is Jealous, is a jealous God.

EXODUS 34:14

That is a very wonderful and suggestive expression: "a jealous God." See that it be engraved on your hearts. Jesus will not endure it that those of us who love Him should divide our hearts between Him and something else. The love which is strong as death is linked with "a jealousy cruel as the grave; its flames are flames of fire, a most vehement flame" (Song of Solomon 8:6).

The royal word to the spouse is, "Forget your own people also, and your father's house; so the King will greatly desire your beauty; because He is your Lord, worship Him" (Psalm 45:10–11). Of course, beloved, the Master never condemns that proper natural affection which we are bound to give, and which is a part of our sanctification to give in its due and proper proportion to those who are related to us. Besides, we are bound to love all the saints, and all mankind in their proper place and measure. But there is a love which is for the Master alone. Inside the heart there must be a *sanctum sanctorum,* within the veil, where He Himself alone must shine like the Shechinah, and reign on the mercy-seat. There must be a glorious high throne within our spirits, where the true Solomon alone must sit; the lions of watchful zeal must guard each step of it. There must He, the King in His beauty, sit enthroned, sole monarch of the heart's affections.

RESPONDING IN PRAYER

"Lord, I feel undeserving because You are jealous for my love.
As the author describes it, may You be the 'monarch of my heart's
affections' so that You may receive from me what you seek."

Continuing in prayer . . .

_____

_____

_____

_____

_____

We are called by God to many different kinds of love on this earth. How then is our love for God sacred and special and different from these earthly loves?

_____

_____

_____

_____

_____

_____

_____

_____

_____

_____

SPIRITUAL GOALS FOR THE WEEK

_____

_____

_____

_____

_____

_____

_____

_____

_____

_____

THE AUTUMN OF LIFE

| 42 |

He has made everything beautiful in its time.
ECCLESIASTES 3:11

We are in autumn now, and very likely, instead of prizing the peculiar treasures of autumn, some will despise the peaceful Sabbath of the year, and mournfully compare yon fading leaves to funeral sermons replete with sadness. Such will contrast summer and autumn, and exalt one above another. Now, whoever shall claim precedence for any season, shall have me for an opponent. They are all beautiful in their season, and each excels after its kind. Even thus it is wrong to compare the early zeal of the young Christian with the mature and mellow experience of the older believer, and make preferences. Each is beautiful according to its time.

You, dear young friend, with your intense zeal, are to be commended and imitated; but very much of your fire I am afraid arises from novelty, and you are not so strong as you are earnest; like a newborn river, you are swift in current, but neither deep nor broad. And you, my more advanced friend, who are much tried and buffeted, to you it is not easy to hold on your way under great inward struggles and severe depressions, but your deeper sense of weakness, your firmer grasp of truth, your more intense fellowship with the Lord Jesus in his sufferings, your patience, and your steadfastness, are all lovely in the eyes of the Lord your God.

Be thankful each of you for what you have, for by the grace of God you are what you are.

RESPONDING IN PRAYER

*"Lord, help me to experience every stage of life as a gift from You
and realize that aging is simply a maturation process
that means we are growing more like You over time."*

Continuing in prayer . . .

_____

_____

_____

_____

_____

Do you unconsciously buy into the world's philosophy that youth is to be prized above age? Write down the benefits in the Christian life of the aging process and compare it to the pleasure of autumn.

_____

_____

_____

_____

_____

_____

_____

_____

_____

_____

_____

SPIRITUAL GOALS FOR THE WEEK

_____

_____

_____

_____

_____

_____

_____

_____

POWER OVER THE WILL

43

So then it is not of him who wills,
nor of him who runs, but of God who shows mercy.

ROMANS 9:16

*S*ome boast of free will. I wonder whether those who believe in it have any more power over persons' wills than I have? I know I have not any. I find the old proverb very true, "One man can bring a horse to the water, but a hundred cannot make him drink." I find that I can bring you all to the water, and a great many more than can get into this chapel; but I cannot make you drink; and I don't think a hundred ministers could make you drink. I have read old Rowland Hill, and Whitfield, and several others, to see what they did; but I cannot discover a plan of turning your wills. I cannot coax you, and you will not yield by any manner of means.

I do not think any man has power over his fellow-creature's will, but the Spirit of God has. He makes the unwilling sinner so willing that he is impetuous after the Gospel; he who was obstinate now hurries to the Cross. He who laughed at Jesus now hangs on His mercy; and he who would not believe is now made by the Holy Spirit to do it, not only willingly, but eagerly; he is happy, is glad to do it, rejoices in the sound of Jesus' name, and delights to run in the way of God's commandments. The Holy Spirit has power over the will.

RESPONDING IN PRAYER

"Lord, thank You that though on my own I cannot will to repent,
You, by the power of Your Holy Spirit, can transform my will
to not only want to receive You but obey You as well."

Continuing in prayer . . .

_____

_____

_____

_____

_____

What hope and comfort is found in the thought that God first chose us rather than our choosing Him? How does this give us a greater chance of perseverance in difficult circumstances?

_____

_____

_____

_____

_____

_____

_____

_____

_____

_____

SPIRITUAL GOALS FOR THE WEEK

_____

_____

_____

_____

_____

_____

_____

_____

_____

REMEMBERED PRAYERS

---44---

Now when He had taken the scroll, the four living creatures and
the twenty-four elders fell down before the Lamb, each having a harp,
and golden bowls full of incense, which are the prayers of the saints.
REVELATION 5:8

Prayers are noticed in heaven. Oh, I know what is the case with many of you. You think, "If I turn to God, if I seek Him, surely I am so inconsiderable a being, so guilty and vile, that it cannot be imagined He would take any notice of me." My friends, harbor no such heathenish ideas. Our God is no god who sits in one perpetual dream; nor does He clothe Himself in such thick darkness that He cannot see; He is not like Baal who heareth not.

True, He may not regard battles; He cares not for the pomp and pageantry of kings; He listens not to the swell of martial music; He regards not the triumph and the pride of man. But whenever there is a heart big with sorrow, wherever there is an eye suffused with tears, wherever there is a lip quivering with agony, wherever there is a deep groan, or a penitential sigh, the ear of Jehovah is wide open; He marks it down in the registry of His memory. He puts our prayers, like rose leaves, between the pages of His book of remembrance, and when the volume is opened at last, there shall be a precious fragrance springing up therefrom.

Oh, poor sinner, of the blackest and vilest character, thy prayers are heard! Even now God hath said of thee, "Behold, He prayeth."

RESPONDING IN PRAYER

"Lord, it is a great comfort to think that You not only remember but
cherish our every prayer, and even the feelings that accompany them. You
do not look upon our sinfulness but only the attitude of our hearts."

Continuing in prayer . . .

_____

_____

_____

_____

_____

FOR REFLECTION

When have you been discouraged from praying because of a sense of guilt or un-
worthiness? Give this over to God and ask Him to remind you how important
your prayers are to Him.

_____

_____

_____

_____

_____

_____

_____

_____

_____

_____

SPIRITUAL GOALS FOR THE WEEK

_____

_____

_____

_____

_____

_____

_____

_____

_____

GOD'S SECRETS

―――――――― 45 ――――――――

The secret of the Lord is with those who fear Him;
and He will show them His covenant.

PSALM 25:14

*A*ll that [Mary] knew we also may discover. Do you wonder that we should say so? Here is a text to prove it. "The secret of the Lord is with those who fear Him; and He will show them His covenant." Remember the Master's words— "No longer do I call you servants; for a servant does not know what his master is doing; but I have called you friends, for all things that I have heard from My Father I have made known to you" (John 15:15). So blessedly does this Divine Revealer of secrets tell us His heart, that He keeps back nothing which is profitable to us; His own assurance is, "If it were not so, I would have told you."

Does He not this day manifest Himself unto us as He does not unto the world? It is even so; and therefore we will not ignorantly cry out, "Blessed is the womb that bore you," but we will intelligently bless God that, having heard the Word and kept it, we have first of all as true a communion with the Savior as the virgin had, and in the second place as true an acquaintance with the secrets of His heart as she can be supposed to have obtained.

RESPONDING IN PRAYER

"Thank You, Lord, that You are willing to share
Your intimate secrets with me and that I can know
You with the same closeness as the mother of Jesus."

Continuing in prayer . . .

_____

_____

_____

_____

_____

_____

_____

FOR REFLECTION

What "secrets" about Himself has God revealed to you recently that have brought you great joy and comfort?

_____
_____
_____
_____
_____
_____
_____
_____
_____
_____
_____

SPIRITUAL GOALS FOR THE WEEK

_____
_____
_____
_____
_____
_____
_____
_____
_____
_____

THE QUALIFICATION OF WEAKNESS

|46|

"This is the word of the Lord to Zerubbabel:
'Not by might nor by power, but by My Spirit,' says the Lord of Hosts.'"
ZECHARIAH 4:6

A primary qualification for serving God with any amount of success, and for doing God's work well and triumphantly, is a sense of our own weakness. When God's warrior marches forth to battle, strong in his own might, when he boasts, "I know that I shall conquer, my own right arm and my conquering sword shall get unto me the victory," defeat is not far distant. God will not go forth with that man who marches in his own strength. He who reckons on victory thus has reckoned wrongly, for it is "not by might nor by power, but by my Spirit, says the Lord Almighty." They who go forth to fight, boasting of their prowess, shall return with their gay banners trailed in the dust and their armor stained with disgrace. Those who serve God must serve Him in His own way, and in His strength, or He will never accept their service.

That which man does, unaided by divine strength, God can never own. The mere fruits of the earth He casts away; He will only reap that corn, the seed of which was sown from heaven, watered by grace, and ripened by the sun of divine love. God will empty out all that thou hast before He will put His own into thee; He will first clean out thy granaries before He will fill them with the finest of the wheat.

RESPONDING IN PRAYER

"More and more, Lord, I realize how weak I am
apart from Your grace. Help me not to presume that
I can do it on my own and ask You to bless it afterwards."

Continuing in prayer . . .

_____

_____

_____

_____

_____

_____

What needs to be "cleaned out of your granaries" before God can produce an abundance of wheat in your life?

_____

_____

_____

_____

_____

_____

_____

_____

_____

_____

SPIRITUAL GOALS FOR THE WEEK

_____

_____

_____

_____

_____

_____

_____

_____

_____

RESURRECTION POWER

47
---

*"That I may know Him and the power of His resurrection,
and the fellowship of His sufferings."*
PHILIPPIANS 3:10

I would have you *believe* that Christ rose from the dead so as to sing of it, and derive all the consolation which it is possible for you to extract from this well-ascertained and well-witnessed fact; but I beseech you, rest not contented even there. Though you cannot, like the disciples, see Him visibly, yet I bid you aspire to see Christ Jesus by the eye of faith; and though, like Mary Magdalene, you may not "touch" Him, yet may you be privileged to converse with Him, and to know that He is risen, you yourselves being risen in Him to newness of life.

To know a crucified Savior as having crucified all my sins, is a high degree of knowledge; but to know a risen Savior as having justified me, and to realize that He has bestowed upon me new life, having given me to be a new creature through His own newness of life, this is a noble style of experience: short of it, none ought to rest satisfied. May you both "know Him, and the power of His resurrection."

Why should souls who are quickened with Jesus, wear the grave clothes of worldliness and unbelief? Rise, for the Lord is risen.

RESPONDING IN PRAYER

*"Lord, with the eyes of faith let me behold You as risen and then
see myself as risen by the same power and having the same nature."*

Continuing in prayer . . .

_____

_____

_____

_____

_____

_____

_____

Do you perceive Jesus more as a crucified Savior who died for your sins or a risen Lord who grants you new life? What does it mean to you to walk in newness of life?

_____

_____

_____

_____

_____

_____

_____

_____

_____

_____

SPIRITUAL GOALS FOR THE WEEK

_____

_____

_____

_____

_____

_____

_____

_____

GOD'S EXPLOITS

---48---

Fear not, for I am with you; Be not dismayed,
for I am your God. I will strengthen you, Yes, I will help you,
I will uphold you with my righteous right hand.

ISAIAH 41:10

*T*hink not that the strength of man shall ever be able to overcome the power of God. While the earth's huge pillars stand, you have enough reason to abide firm in your faith. The same God who directs the earth in its orbit, who feeds the burning furnace of the sun, and trims the lamps of heaven, has promised to supply you with daily strength. While He is able to uphold the universe, dream not that He will prove unable to fulfill His own promises.

Remember what He did in the days of old, in the former generations. Remember how He spoke and it was done; how He commanded, and it stood fast. Shall He that created the world grow weary? He hangs the world upon nothing; shall He who does this be unable to support His children? Shall He be unfaithful to His word for want of power? Who is it that restrains the tempest? Does not He ride upon the wings of the wind, and make the clouds His chariots, and hold the ocean in the hollow of His hand? How can He fail thee?

When He has put such a faithful promise as this on record, will you for a moment indulge the thought that He has outpromised Himself, and gone beyond His power to fulfill? Ah, no! You cannot doubt any longer.

RESPONDING IN PRAYER

"Lord, it is good to be reminded that You never fail us,
being the powerful God You are. Help us to trust You
even when the odds are overwhelming or You seem absent."

Continuing in prayer . . .

_____

_____

_____

_____

_____

FOR REFLECTION

What promises in Scripture can you find that talk about God's strength and fruit-fulness on your behalf?

_____

_____

_____

_____

_____

_____

_____

_____

_____

_____

SPIRITUAL GOALS FOR THE WEEK

_____

_____

_____

_____

_____

_____

_____

_____

_____

A DIVIDING SWORD

---49---

"Do not think that I came to bring peace to the earth.
I did not come to bring peace but a sword."

MATTHEW 10:34

*O*h, you who have taken up His cross, have you not heard what your Master said? "I have come to 'set a man against his father, a daughter against her mother, and a daughter-in-law against her mother-in-law.' And 'a man's foe will be those of his own household.'" Christ is the great Peacemaker; but before peace, He brings war. Where the light comes, the darkness must return. Where truth is, the lie must flee; or, if it abides, there must be a stern conflict, for the truth cannot and will not lower its standard, and the lie must be trodden under foot.

If you follow Christ, you shall have all the dogs of the world yelping at your heels. If you would live so as to stand the test of the last tribunal, depend upon it, the world will not speak well of you. He who has the friendship of the world is an enemy to God; but if you are true and faithful to the Most High, men will resent your unflinching fidelity, since it is a testimony against their iniquities. Fearless of all consequences, you must do the right. You will need the courage of a lion unhesitatingly to pursue a course which shall turn your best friend into your fiercest foe; but for the love of Jesus you must thus be courageous.

RESPONDING IN PRAYER

"Lord, take Your sword and cut through the darkness
and worldliness in my own life. Help me to stand firmly
and courageously for You where it counts."

Continuing in prayer . . .

_____

_____

_____

_____

_____

_____

When has the message of the Gospel produced opposition in your own life
where it has cost you to take a stand?

_____

_____

_____

_____

_____

_____

_____

_____

_____

_____

SPIRITUAL GOALS FOR THE WEEK

_____

_____

_____

_____

_____

_____

_____

_____

_____

TALENT TO USE

"Give and it shall be given to you: good measure, pressed down, shaken together, and running over will be put into your bosom."

LUKE 6:38

*W*hen the feast was finished, there were fragments to be gathered. This is a part of the history of the loaves—they were eaten, but they were there; people were filled with them, but yet there was more of them left than when the feast began. Each disciple had a basketful to carry back to his Master's feet. Give yourself to Christ, and when you have used yourself for His glory, you will be more able to serve Him than you are now; you shall find your little stock grow as you spend it. Remember Bunyan's picture of the man who had a roll of cloth. He unrolled it, and he cut off so much for the poor. Then he unrolled it, and cut off some more, and the more he cut it, the longer it grew.

It is certainly so with talent and ability, and with grace in the heart. The more you use it, the more there is of it. It is often so with gold and silver; the store of the liberal man increases, while the miser grows poor. We have an old proverb, which is as true as it is suggestive: "Drawn wells have the sweetest waters." So, if you keep continually drawing on your mind, your thoughts will get sweeter; and if you continue to draw on your strength, your strength will get to be more mighty through God. The more you do, the more you may do, by the grace of the Ever-blessed One!

RESPONDING IN PRAYER

Lord, let me remember that when I give it will be given to me in much greater abundance. Help me to be liberal with what I have so that others may benefit and my storehouse too will increase."

Continuing in prayer . . .

_____

_____

_____

_____

_____

FOR REFLECTION

Search the Scriptures and/or church history for individuals who have been given more because they gave to God. What principles do you glean?

_____

_____

_____

_____

_____

_____

_____

_____

_____

SPIRITUAL GOALS FOR THE WEEK

_____

_____

_____

_____

_____

_____

_____

_____

_____

_____

_____

_____

PLENTY OF GRACE

---|51|---

I will make them and the places all around My hill a blessing; and I will cause showers to come down in their season; there shall be showers of blessing.
EZEKIEL 34:26

*Wh*o can say, "I will give them showers," except God? There is only one voice which can speak to the clouds, and bid them beget the rain. "Who sends down the rain upon the earth? Who scatters the showers upon the green herb? Do not I, the Lord?" So grace is the gift of God and is not to be created by man.

It is also *needed* grace. What would the ground do without showers? You may break the clods, you may sow your seeds, but what can you do without the rain? As absolutely needful is the divine blessing. In vain you labor, until God the plenteous shower bestows, and sends salvation down.

Then it is *plenteous* grace. "I will send them showers." It does not say, "I will send them drops," but "showers." So it is with grace. If God gives a blessing, He usually gives it in such a measure that there is not room enough to receive it. Plenteous grace! Ah! We want plenteous grace to keep us humble, to make us prayerful, to make us holy; plenteous grace to make us zealous, to preserve us through this life, and at last to land us in heaven. We cannot do without saturating showers of grace.

RESPONDING IN PRAYER

"Lord, please pour out Your grace upon me until there is no more room to receive it because I need it for everything in my life that pleases You."

Continuing in prayer . . .

_____

_____

_____

_____

_____

_____

FOR REFLECTION

The above passage lists three elements of God's grace. Name some aspects of your
spiritual life where God's help is needed.

_____

_____

_____

_____

_____

_____

_____

_____

_____

_____

SPIRITUAL GOALS FOR THE WEEK

_____

_____

_____

_____

_____

_____

_____

_____

LEARNING HOW TO BE FULL

I know how to be abased, and I know how to abound.
Everywhere and in all things I have learned both to be full
and to be hungry, both to abound and to suffer need.
PHILIPPIANS 4:12

The apostle tells us that he knew how to abound. When Paul had much, he knew how to use it. Abundant grace enabled him to bear abundant prosperity. When he had a full sail he was loaded with much ballast, and so floated safely. It needs more than human skill to carry the brimming cup of mortal joy with a steady hand, yet Paul had learned that skill, for he declares, "In all things I have learned both to be full and to be hungry."

It is a divine lesson to know how to be full, for the Israelites were full once, but while the flesh was yet in their mouth, the wrath of God came upon them. Many have asked for mercies that they might satisfy their own hearts' lust. Fullness of bread has often made fullness of blood, and that has brought on wantonness of spirit. When we have much of God's providential mercies, it often happens that we have but little of God's grace, and little gratitude for the bounties we have received. We are full and we forget God: satisfied with earth, we are content to do without heaven. Rest assured it is harder to know how to be full than it is to know how to be hungry—so desperate is the tendency of human nature to pride and forgetfulness of God.

Take care that you ask in your prayers that God would teach you "how to be full."

RESPONDING IN PRAYER

"Lord, help me to be content with Your divine providence in my life,
whether You give me little or much. I know I can prosper
in my spirit because it is sufficient for me."

Continuing in prayer . . .

When in your life has having too little or too much taken you further from the Lord? How can you thrive on both a little or a lot in the material realm without it removing trust in God?

_____

_____

_____

_____

_____

_____

_____

_____

_____

SPIRITUAL GOALS FOR THE WEEK

_____

_____

_____

_____

_____

_____

_____

_____

JAMES S. BELL, JR. serves as acquisitions manager at Moody Press and has received cover credit for more than fifteen books that he compiled, edited, or introduced. His specialty is classic literature, inclusing revisions of *Quo Vadis* and *Ben Hur.* He lives in West Chicago with his wife, Margaret, and children: Rosheen, Brendan, Brigit, and Caitlin.